OFFICIAL

Updated
Second Edition

T0384688

Workbook 2
with Online Resources
American English

Caroline Nixon & Michael Tomlinson

Cambridge University Press
www.cambridge.org/elt

Cambridge Assessment English
www.cambridgeenglish.org

Information on this title: www.cambridge.org/9781316627174

© Cambridge University Press & Assessment 2008, 2015, 2017

First published 2008
Second edition 2015
Updated second edition 2017

40 39 38 37 36 35 34 33 32 31 30 29 28 27 26 25 24 23 22 21 20

Printed in the Netherlands by Wilco BV

A catalog record for this publication is available from the British Library

ISBN 978-1-316-62717-4 Workbook with Online Resources 2
ISBN 978-1-316-62751-8 Student's Book 2
ISBN 978-1-316-62701-3 Teacher's Book 2
ISBN 978-1-316-62734-1 Teacher's Resource Book with Online Audio 2
ISBN 978-1-316-62723-5 Class Audio CDs 2 (4 CDs)
ISBN 978-1-316-62578-1 Flashcards 2
ISBN 978-1-316-62788-4 Interactive DVD with Teacher's Booklet 2 (PAL/NTSC)
ISBN 978-1-316-62709-9 Presentation Plus 2
ISBN 978-1-316-63016-7 Posters 2
ISBN 978-1-316-62698-6 Monty's Alphabet Book

Additional resources for this publication at www.cambridge.org/elt/kidsboxamericanenglish

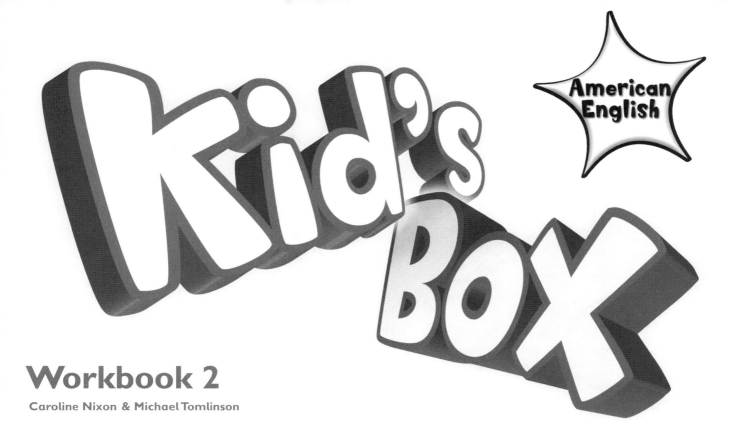

Kid's Box

American English

Workbook 2

Caroline Nixon & Michael Tomlinson

 # Hi again!

1 ✏️ Write.

I'm Sally.

I'm Scott.

I'm Suzy.

Hi, I'm Grandma Star. This is my family.

She's _Sally._ He's _____ _____

 I'm Mr. Star.

I'm Mrs. Star.

I'm Grandpa

_____ _____ _____

2 ✏️ Draw and write.

What's your name? **Me!**

_____

How old are you?

_____

3 ✏️ Color the stars.

(1) ⭐⭐☆☆☆☆☆☆☆☆
Color two stars.

(2) ☆☆☆☆☆☆☆☆☆☆
Color five stars.

(3) ☆☆☆☆☆☆☆☆☆☆
Color six stars.

(4) ☆☆☆☆☆☆☆☆☆☆
Color one star.

(5) ☆☆☆☆☆☆☆☆☆☆
Color eight stars.

4 ✏️ Match and connect.

(1)	four + one =	7		eight
(2)	two + one =	5		seven
(3)	six + one =	8		five
(4)	eight + one =	6		ten
(5)	five + one =	9		six
(6)	seven + one =	10		three
(7)	nine + one =	3		nine

5 🔊 ✏️ Listen and color.

6 🔊 ✏️ Listen and point. Write the words.

lylaS   Szuy   ctoSt   frou   igteh   sneev

① This is __Sally.__
She's __eight.__

② This is _____
He's _____

③ This is _____
She's _____

7 Read the question. Listen and write a name or a number.
There are two examples.

Example

What is the boy's name? _____ Dan _____

How old is he? _____ 9 _____

Questions

① What is the girl's name? _____

② How old is the girl? _____

③ What is the name of Dan's street? _____
Street

④ What number is Dan's house? _____

⑤ What is the name of Grace's book? _____
House

8 🔊 11 CD1 ✏️ Listen and complete.

1. black
2. g_m_
3. s_y
4. b_g
5. c_t
6. pl_y
7. h_nd
8. sn_k_
9. gr_y
10. _pple

9 🔊 12 CD1 ✏️ Listen and write. Match.

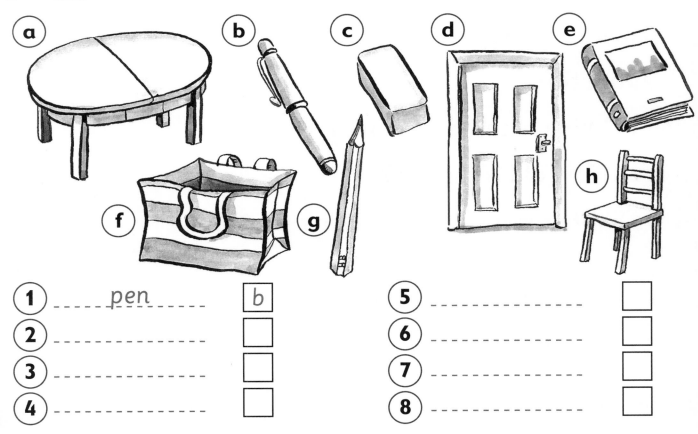

1. ____pen____ | b |
2. _____ | |
3. _____ | |
4. _____ | |
5. _____ | |
6. _____ | |
7. _____ | |
8. _____ | |

My picture dictionary

  Listen and write. Stick.

① _purple_	②	③
④	⑤	⑥

My progress

 Check (✓) or put an **X**.

I can count to ten. ☐

I can say the colors. ☐

I can say the alphabet. ☐

2 Back to school

1 🔍✏️ **Find and write the words.**

desk

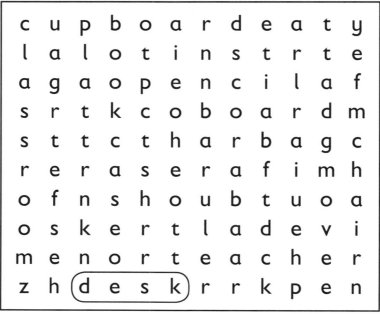

```
c u p b o a r d e a t y
l a l o t i n s t r t e
a g a o p e n c i l a f
s r t k c o b o a r d m
s t t c t h a r b a g c
r e r a s e r a f i m h
o f n s h o u b t u o a
o s k e r t l a d e v i
m e n o r t e a c h e r
z h (d e s k) r r k p e n
```

2 ▶️18 CD1 ✏️ **Listen and color.**

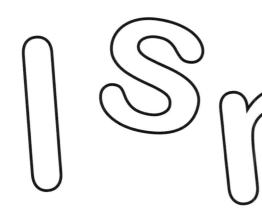  

3  Look at the numbers. Write the words.

veleen
11

eleven

niffeet
15

----

hiegeetn
18

----

ewletv
12

----

wytent
20

----

reihtnet
13

----

4 Read and color.

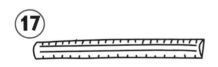

Color number twelve brown.
Color number nineteen pink.
Color number fourteen green.
Color number seventeen blue.
Color number sixteen orange.

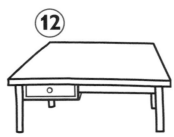

5 ✏️ **Write the sentences.**

1 (a ruler) (There's) (the table.) (on)

There's a ruler on the table.

2 (the desk.) (There are) (on) (12 pencils)

----

3 (There's) (under) (the chair.) (a backpack)

----

4 (the bookcase.) (16 books) (in) (There are)

----

6 🔍✏️ **Look at the picture. Write the answers**

1 How many burgers are there? _There are six._

2 How many apples are there? _____

3 How many oranges are there? _____

4 How many cupcakes are there? _____

5 How many ice-cream cones are there? _____

6 How many bananas are there? _____

 Look and read. Write "yes" or "no."

Examples

There are two teachers in the classroom.   _no_

There's a poster on the wall.   _yes_

Questions

① There is a door next to the cupboard.   _____

② There is a board on the wall.   _____

③ There are two tables under the board.   _____

④ There is a ruler on a bookcase.   _____

⑤ There are three cars under the desk.   _____

# 8 25 CD1 ✏ Listen and color red or green.

① red

② green

③ tree

④ 10 ten

⑤ pen

⑥ read

⑦ 12 twelve

⑧ 14 fourteen

⑨ teacher

⑩ desk

9 🔍 ✏ Find the words.

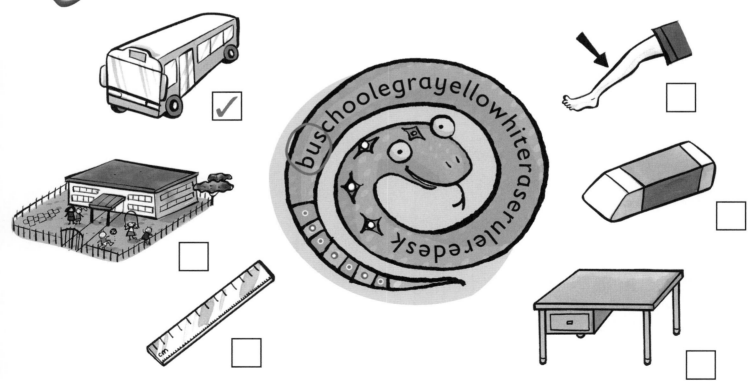

buschoolegrayellowhiteraserulleredesk

How many colors are there? _____

What are they? _____

My picture dictionary

  Write the words. Stick.

taechre	baodr	rlure
teacher	_ _ _ _ _ _ _ _	_ _ _ _ _ _ _ _
skde	bkoocsae	cpubaord
_ _ _ _ _ _ _ _	_ _ _ _ _ _ _ _	_ _ _ _ _ _ _ _

My progress

Check (✓) or put an X.

I can talk about my classroom. ☐

I can say the numbers 11–20. ☐

I can spell. ☐

Now you! 1 💬✏️ **Ask and answer. Color the graph.**

Which animals do you like?

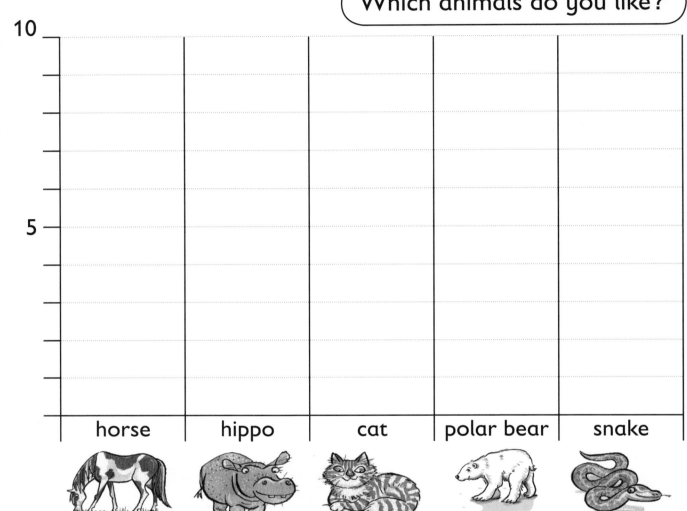

| | horse | hippo | cat | polar bear | snake |

2 🔍✏️ **Answer the questions.**

1 How many children like horses? _ _ _ _ _ _ _ _ _ _

2 How many children like hippos? _ _ _ _ _ _ _ _ _ _

3 How many children like cats? _ _ _ _ _ _ _ _ _ _

4 How many children like polar bears? _ _ _ _ _ _ _ _ _ _

5 How many children like snakes? _ _ _ _ _ _ _ _ _ _

3 Read and complete.

| come in | Yes, of course. | After you. | Can you spell |

1

— Can we _____come in_____, please?
— Yes, come in.

2

— _____
— Thank you.

3

— _____
ruler, please?
— Yes, r-u-l-e-r.

4

— Can you open the window, please?
— _____

4 Draw a picture of you. Be polite!

 Me!

3 Play time!

1 🔍✏️ **Read. Circle the "toy" words. Write.**

k i t e

_____ ____

_____

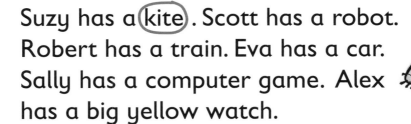
Suzy has a (kite). Scott has a robot.
Robert has a train. Eva has a car.
Sally has a computer game. Alex
has a big yellow watch.

____ _____

2 🔊33 CD1 ✏️ **Listen and check (✓) the box.**

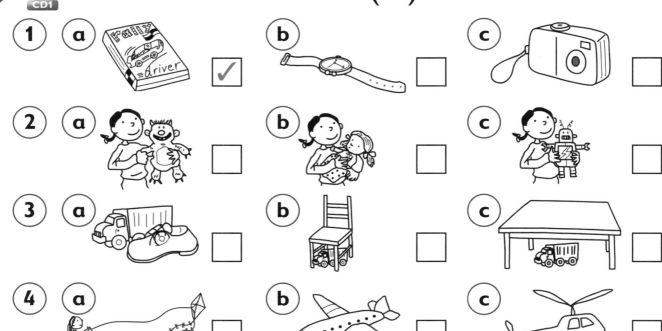

3 ✏️ Complete the sentences and color the pictures.

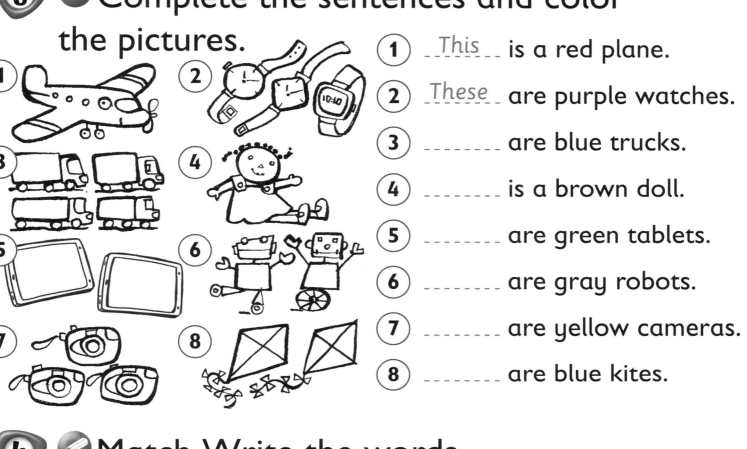

1 _This_ is a red plane.

2 _These_ are purple watches.

3 _____ are blue trucks.

4 _____ is a brown doll.

5 _____ are green tablets.

6 _____ are gray robots.

7 _____ are yellow cameras.

8 _____ are blue kites.

4 ✏️ Match. Write the words.

k	_kitchen_	_kite_	~~itchen~~	obot
c	_____	_____	amera	ain
r	_____	_____	uler	~~ite~~
d	_____	_____	oll	ane
tr	_____	_____	uck	og
pl	_____	_____	ease	ake

19

5 🔊 38 CD1 ✏️ Listen and color. Then answer.

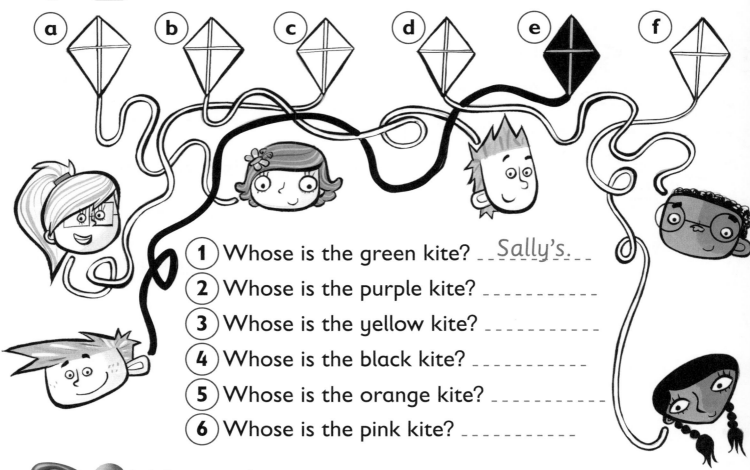

(a) (b) (c) (d) (e) (f)

(1) Whose is the green kite? _Sally's._
(2) Whose is the purple kite? _ _ _ _ _ _ _ _ _ _
(3) Whose is the yellow kite? _ _ _ _ _ _ _ _ _ _
(4) Whose is the black kite? _ _ _ _ _ _ _ _ _ _
(5) Whose is the orange kite? _ _ _ _ _ _ _ _ _ _
(6) Whose is the pink kite? _ _ _ _ _ _ _ _ _ _

6 ✏️ Write the questions.

(1) _Whose is the truck?_ _ _ _ _ _ _ _ It's Bill's.
(2) _ _ _ _ _ _ _ _ _ _ _ _ _ _ _ _ _ _ _ It's Lucy's.
(3) _ _ _ _ _ _ _ _ _ _ _ _ _ _ _ _ _ _ _ It's Ben's.
(4) _ _ _ _ _ _ _ _ _ _ _ _ _ _ _ _ _ _ _ It's Kim's.
(5) _ _ _ _ _ _ _ _ _ _ _ _ _ _ _ _ _ _ _ It's Tony's.

7 Look and read. Put a ✓ or an ✗ in the box. There is one example.

Examples

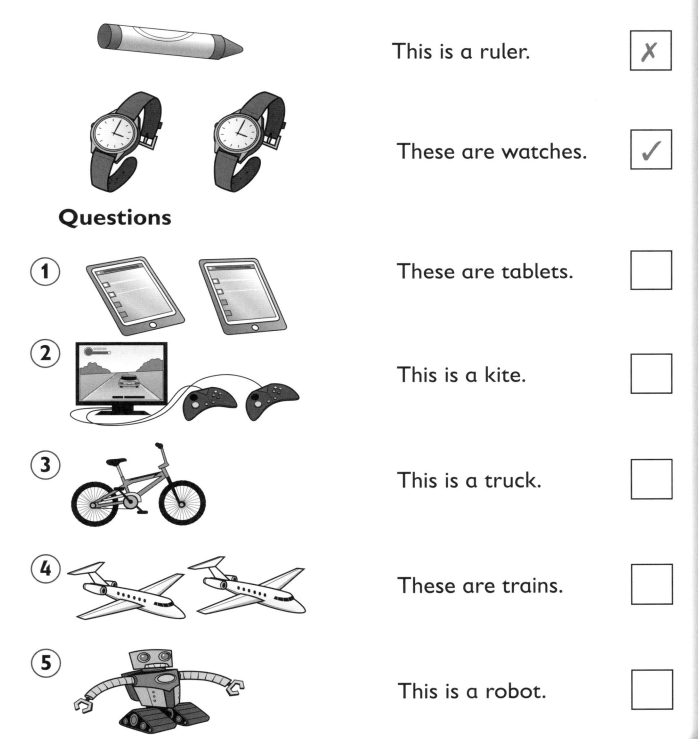

This is a ruler. ✗

These are watches. ✓

Questions

① These are tablets. ☐

② This is a kite. ☐

③ This is a truck. ☐

④ These are trains. ☐

⑤ This is a robot. ☐

8 🔊 42 CD1 ✏️ **Listen and write the words.**

(**1**) ~~fish~~ (**2**) ~~kite~~ (**3**) pink (**4**) five (**5**) my

(**6**) swim (**7**) bike (**8**) big (**9**) fly (**10**) sit

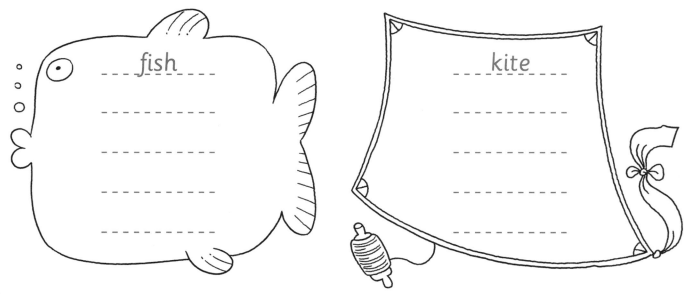

fish

kite

9 🔊 43 CD1 ✏️ **Listen and connect the dots.**

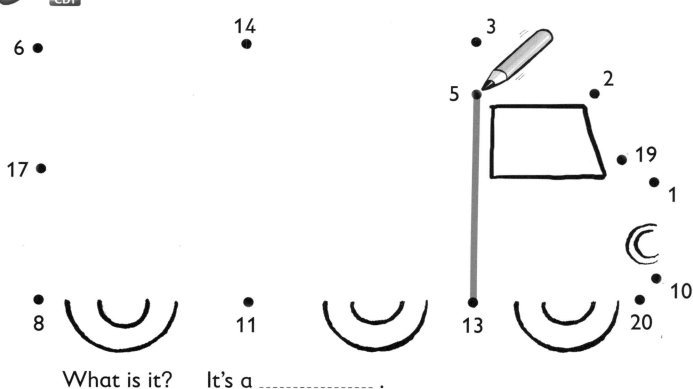

What is it?   It's a _____.

My picture dictionary

  Listen and stick. Write the words.

(1) _kite_	(2)	(3)
(4)	(5)	(6)

My progress

Check (✔) or put an ✗.

I can talk about my favorite toy. ☐

I can write "toy" words. ☐

4 At home

1 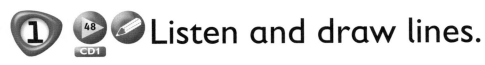 Listen and draw lines.

Bill   Dan   Alice   Eva

Matt   Pat   Lucy

2 Write the words.

³m	a	t				
	6					
			4			
	1					
	7	2		8		
4						
	5					

1	2	3	4	5	6	7	8

24

3 🔍 ✏️ Read and write the number. Draw.

sixteen = __16__ → m

fourteen = _____ → l

seventeen = _____ → r

eighteen = _____ → o

twenty = _____ → p

twelve = _____ → c

fifteen = _____ → a

thirteen = _____ → i

nineteen = _____ → u

eleven = _____ → h

(1)

m					
16	13	17	17	18	17

(2)

14	15	16	20

(3)

12	18	19	12	11

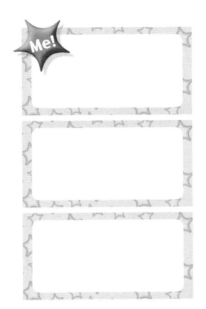

Me!

4 🔍 ✏️ Read and write the words.

| mirror ~~bedroom~~ mat face bath |

My bathroom is next to my (1) _bedroom_. In my bathroom, I
sit in the (2) _____ and wash my body. On the wall, there
is a (3) _____ . You can see your (4) _____ in it.
There is a blue (5) _____ on the floor. You can stand on it.

5 ✏ Write "yours" or "mine."

1 Whose is this?
It's __mine__.

2 Is this _____ or Scott's?
It's mine.

3 Is this _____ ?
Yes, it is.

4 Whose are these?
They're _____.

6 🎵 53 CD1 ✏ Listen and color.

7 Listen and draw lines. There is one example.

Mark   Sue   Kim   Grace

Nick   Hugo   Matt

8 🔊58 CD1 ✏️ Listen and write the words.

(1) ~~boat~~ (2) ~~box~~ (3) doll (4) phone (5) clock

(6) clothes (7) yell<u>ow</u> (8) ro<u>b</u>ot (9) socks (10) old

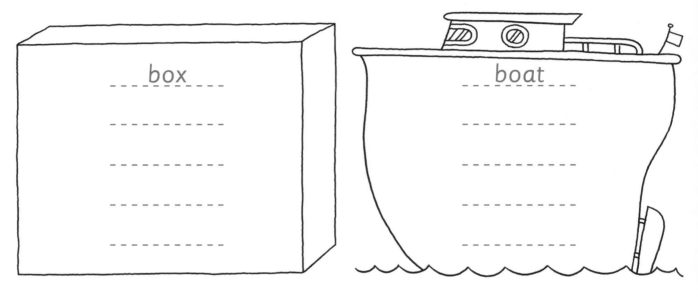

box _ _ _ _ _ _ _ _

boat _ _ _ _ _ _ _ _

9 ✏️ Write the words.

| This | ~~That~~ These Those These That |

(1) _That_ is a couch.

(2) _ _ _ _ _ _ _ _ _ is a phone.

(3) _ _ _ _ _ _ _ _ are armchairs.

(4) _ _ _ _ _ _ _ _ is a clock.

(5) _ _ _ _ _ _ _ _ are rugs.

(6) _ _ _ _ _ _ _ _ are beds.

My picture dictionary

  Complete the words. Stick.

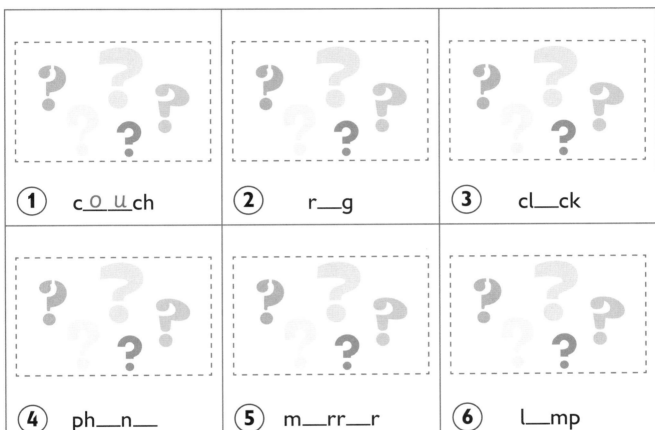

① c_o_u_ch

② r__g

③ cl__ck

④ ph__n__

⑤ m__rr__r

⑥ l__mp

My progress

Check (✓) or put an ✗.

I can talk about my house. ☐

I can say what's mine. ☐

🔍 👤 **Make a jumping frog.**

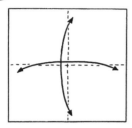 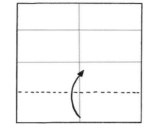 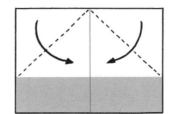 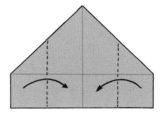

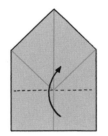 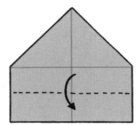 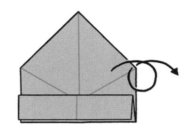 

2 🔍 ✏️ **Look and write.**

~~robot~~ couch cupboard kite phone lamp

1

robot

2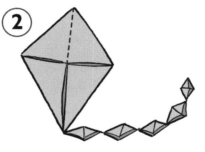

_____

3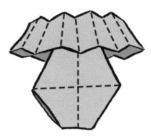

_____

4

_____

5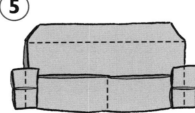

_____

6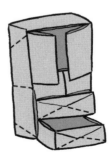

_____

3 🔍 ✏️ Look, read, and match.

①  ② ③ ④

a an old T-shirt **b** an old sock **c** old paper **d** a plastic bottle

4 ✏️ You have four boxes, two socks, a T-shirt, and five pencils. Draw a robot.

Review

1 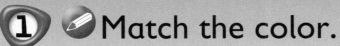 Match the color.

7 gray	nine	**8** yellow	three	**5** pink
6 blue	ten	two	**10** orange	four
five	**3** purple	**9** green	eight	**1** brown
2 red	seven	six	**4** black	one

2 5 CD2 Listen and write the number.

13

32

3 ✏️ Write the questions. Answer the questions.

	a	b	c	d	e	f
1	what	trucks	dirty	how	big	bed
2	shoes	toy	clean	small	balls	whose
3	is	small	camera	many	are	chair
4	there	under	where	on	the	or

1 4c 3e 4e 1b

Where are the trucks _____ ?

_____ .

2 2f 2b 3a 4d 4e 1f

_____ ?

_____ .

3 3e 4e 2a 2c 4f 1c

_____ ?

_____ .

4 1d 3d 1b 3e 4a

_____ ?

_____ .

5 4c 3a 4e 3c

_____ ?

_____ .

6 1a 3a 4d 4e 3f

_____ ?

_____ .

5 Meet my family

1  Read and write the names.

This is Robert and his family. He's with his brother Sam, his sister May, and his cousin Frank. Robert's brother has a big nose. Robert has small eyes. Robert's cousin is young. He's a baby. Robert's sister has long hair.

2 Write the words.

~~couch~~   ~~mom~~   ~~plane~~   ~~bookcase~~   teacher   grandma   baby
kite   desk   truck   grandpa   playground   cousin   rug   robot
board   mirror   boat   lamp   dad   bed   ruler   doll   phone

In the house
couch

Family
mom

Toys
plane

In the school
bookcase

5

3 Read. Write the name. Color.

--------------------- --------------------- --------------------- ---------------------

Hi. This is my family. My mommy has long purple hair, small green ears, and five yellow teeth. Her name's Trudy. My daddy's name's Tom. He has short red hair and a dirty green nose. He has eight brown teeth. My brother Tony has long brown hair, big red eyes, and one white tooth. My sister's name is Tricia. She's very clean! She has big ears, short blue hair, orange eyes, and six green teeth.

4  Write the words.

bbya   afntharedrg   anthmoredrg   oremth

sstire   fthrea   dda   csinou   rthbore   mmo

baby

baby

5 🔟 CD2 ✏️ Listen and write the number.

6 🔍 ✏️ Look at the pictures and write the letters.

1. – What are you doing, Mom?
   – I'm making a cake. `c`
   `d`

2. – Whose kite are you flying, Scott?
   – I'm flying your kite, Suzy.

3. – What are you eating, Dad?
   – I'm eating chocolate ice cream.

4. – Whose shoes are you cleaning, Grandpa?
   – I'm cleaning Scott's shoes.

5. – Which word are you spelling, Sally?
   – I'm spelling "beautiful."

6. – What are you drawing, Grandma?
   – I'm drawing Sally.

7 13 CD2 Listen and check (✓) the box.
There is one example.

Example

What is Dan doing?

Questions

1 Which girl is Anna?

2 What's Sue doing?

3 What's Grandpa doing?

4 What's Sam drawing?

8 🔊15 CD2 ✏️ Listen and write.

1 bu̲s

2 sh___

3 tr_ck

4 S___

5 s_n

6 r_ler

7 bl___

8 r_n

9 j_mp

9 ✏️ Write the letters.

a	He's kicking	his car.	
b	They're cleaning	in her bed.	
c	He's driving	a ball.	a
d	She's sleeping	books.	
e	We're singing	a song.	
f	I'm playing	the guitar.	
g	They're reading	their rooms.	

My picture dictionary

   Listen and write. Stick.

? ? ? ?	? ? ? ?	? ? ? ?
① _grandma_	② _ _ _ _ _ _ _	③ _ _ _ _ _ _ _
? ? ? ?	? ? ? ?	? ? ? ?
④ _ _ _ _ _ _ _	⑤ _ _ _ _ _ _ _	⑥ _ _ _ _ _ _ _

My progress

Check (✓) or put an X.

I can talk about my family. ☐

I can talk about actions. ☐

39

6 Dinner time

1 🔍✏️ Read the lists and find the food.

Draw lines with a pencil.

Draw lines with a pen.

a Shopping list

- oranges
- bread
- rice
- bananas
- apples
- milk
- ice cream
- burgers
- apple juice
- eggs
- water

b Shopping list

- potatoes
- rice
- bread
- carrots
- fish
- orange juice
- fries
- chicken
- lemons
- meat

 **2** Find and color.

Color the pears green.
Color the carrots orange.
Color the tomatoes red.

Color the chicken brown.
Color the meat red.
Color the lemons yellow.

3 Draw and write about your favorite food. Ask and answer.

Me!

What's your favorite food for dinner?

It's chicken and fries.

My favorite food is _____

_____

_____

_____

_____

4 **25** **CD2** Listen and check (✓) or put an ✗.

① ✗

②

③

④

5 Read and write the numbers.

Here you are. ☐

Can I have some juice, please? 1

Orange juice, please. ☐

Which juice – orange juice or apple juice? ☐

Which fruit – a banana, a pear, or an apple? ☐

Here you are. ☐

Can I have some fruit, please? ☐

A pear, please. ☐

6 🔍✏️ Read and choose a word from the box. Write the word next to numbers 1–5. There is one example.

My breakfast

I eat my breakfast in the __kitchen__ . I sit on a (1) _____ at the table. My dad and my (2) _____ sit with me. My favorite drink for breakfast is (3) _____ , and I eat an (4) _____ with lots of bread. I don't like fruit. My dad loves fruit, and he has two (5) _____ every morning for his breakfast.

Example

~~kitchen~~   egg   bananas   lunch

mirrors   chair   milk   brother

7   Listen and write the words.

| teacher | chair | watch | ~~children~~ | chicken | kitchen | lunch | chocolate |

1 children

2

3

4

5

6

7

8

8 Write the words and the letters.

a

b

c

d

e

f

g

h

1 gegs _____eggs_____ | g |

2 lmki _____ | |

3 sefir _____ | |

4 eirc _____ | |

5 tarew _____ | |

6 batsmelal _____ | |

7 ceuji _____ | |

8 radbe _____ | |

My picture dictionary

9 Write the words. Stick.

ckinehc	gegs	rifes
chicken	_ _ _ _ _ _ _	_ _ _ _ _ _ _

lkmi	rcie	dearb
_ _ _ _ _ _ _	_ _ _ _ _ _ _	_ _ _ _ _ _ _

My progress

Check (✓) or put an X.

I can talk about my favorite food. ☐

I can talk about breakfast, lunch, ☐
and dinner.

I can ask and answer questions ☐
about food.

Marie's science   Food

1 **Read and match.**

| milk | meatballs | eggs | lemons | potatoes | carrots |

Now you! 2  **Write the words.**

| apples   potatoes   milk   carrots   eggs   lemons
meat   chicken   oranges   rice   pears   tomatoes |

From animals …   From plants …   From trees …

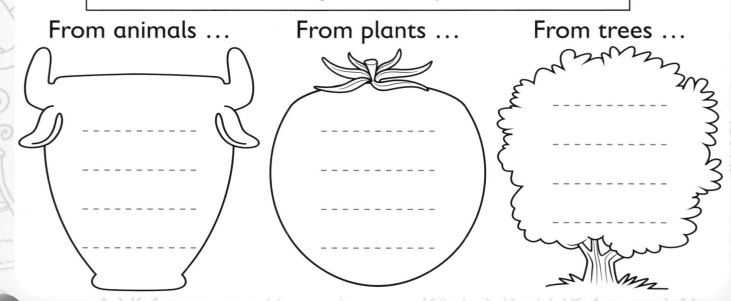

3 Draw your favorite food.

| milk | bread | eggs | juice | chicken | rice | water | fish |
| carrots | apples | meatballs | potatoes | bananas | oranges |

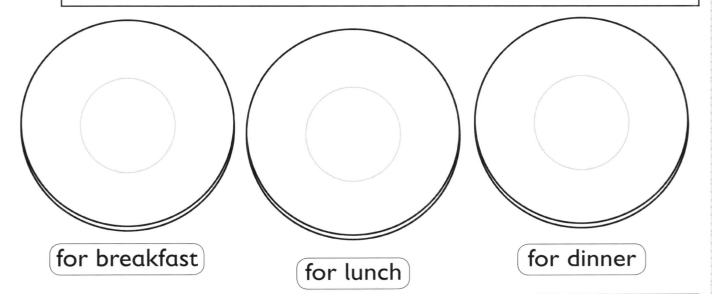

for breakfast

for lunch

for dinner

4 Now tell your partner.
Draw your friend's food.

What's your favorite food for breakfast?

I like oranges and apples.

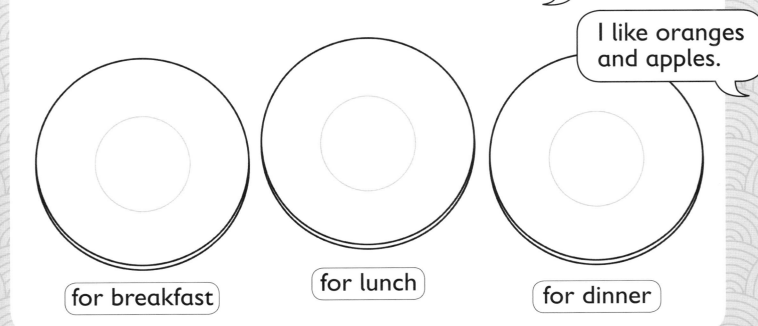

for breakfast

for lunch

for dinner

7 On the farm

1 🔍✏️ Find and write the words.

```
w a l e r s d s p i
s h e e p t u p l d
e d m e y k c i r a
p m i u s a k d b y
t h c h i c k e n a
e w t o g o y r o b
c a s r z w i l s i
h f i s h e t r h r
a r t e l i z a r d
m o u s e f r e n d
s g o a t r f r e v
```

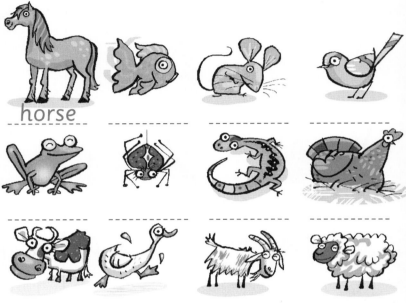

horse

2 🔍✏️ Read. Draw and write the words.

~~snakes~~ ~~crocodiles~~ fish   lizards   birds   giraffes   tigers   monkeys

This is the Star Zoo. The birds are next to the snakes. The fish are under the birds. The lizards are between the fish and the monkeys. The yellow and brown animals next to the monkeys are giraffes. The big orange and black cats under the crocodiles are tigers.

snakes

crocodiles

3  Draw lines.

 Now ask your friend and draw lines.

Where is the donkey? It's in the cupboard.

4 (38 CD2) ✏️ **Write the words. Listen and check.**

~~love~~   I   So   do   I   love   lizards   don't

1
a I _love_ spiders.

b So do _____ .

2
c _____ love fish.

d _____ do I.

3
e I love _____ .

f So _____ I.

4
g I _____ goats.

h I _____ .

5 ✏️💬 **Draw your favorite animal.**
Ask your friend.

What's your favorite animal?

Me!

I love _____ .

6 Listen and color. There is one example.

7   Listen and write.

1  _sp_ider

2 ___ar

3 ___ake

4 ___im

5 ___irt

6 ___ow

7 ___orts

8 ____ool

8 Write the "animal" words.

¹s
p
i
d
e
r

Down

1 This is small and black, and it has eight legs.

2 We get eggs from this farm bird.

6 This farm animal can eat clothes.

Across

1 This farm animal has white hair.

2 We get milk from this big farm animal.

3 This green or brown animal has four short legs, a long body, and a long thin tail.

4 This bird has orange feet. It can swim.

5 This small green animal has big feet and long legs. It can swim and jump.

7 This big animal has big ears.

My picture dictionary

 9 Listen and stick. Write the words.

? ? ? ? ?	? ? ? ? ?	? ? ? ? ?
① _spider_	② _____	③ _____
? ? ? ? ?	? ? ? ? ?	? ? ? ? ?
④ _____	⑤ _____	⑥ _____

My progress

Check (✔) or put an ✗.

I can write "animal" words. ☐

I can talk about things I love. ☐

8 My town

1 🔍✏️ **Look and read. Check (✓) or put an ✗ in the box.**

 (1) This is an apartment. ✗

 (2) These are boots. ☐

 (3) This is a hospital. ☐

 (4) This is a street. ☐

 (5) This is a park. ☐

 (6) This is a café. ☐

2 ✏️ **Circle the different word.**

(1)	car	truck	bus	(boot)
(2)	apartment	town	goat	street
(3)	bike	café	hospital	school
(4)	kitchen	bedroom	bathroom	park
(5)	store	cupboard	armchair	couch
(6)	street	park	school	bedroom
(7)	frog	hospital	café	apartment
(8)	door	town	window	floor

3 🔍 ✏️ Spot the differences.

① In A _there's one car_ , but in B _there are two cars_ .

② In A _____ , but in B _____ .

③ In A _____ , but in B _____ .

④ In A _____ , but in B _____ .

⑤ In A _____ , but in B _____ .

⑥ In A _____ , but in B _____ .

4 ✏️ Write the words.

~~skateboard~~ ~~pear~~ ~~chair~~ ~~dog~~ coconut armchair table bike
apple computer game lizard pineapple cat train car lemon
truck fish mouse mirror clock orange bird cupboard

RED'S FRUIT

pear
_____
_____
_____
_____

TED'S TOYS

skateboard
_____
_____
_____
_____
_____

Pete's Pets

dog
_____
_____
_____
_____
_____

Phil's Furniture

chair
_____
_____
_____
_____

5  Listen and color the stars.

1 2 3
4 5 6
7 8 9

6 Read and write the names.

Tom

You're Tom. You're sitting in front of Jill.
You're Ann. You're sitting between Tom and Nick.
You're Bill. You're sitting behind Nick.
You're Sue. You're sitting between Jill and Bill.

7  Look at the pictures and read the questions. Write one-word answers.

Examples

Where are the people?   at a _____ café _____

How many children are there?   _____ two _____

Questions

① Where is the dog?   under the _____

② What does the boy have?   some _____

③ What is the dog doing?   _____

④ Who is sad?   the _____

⑤ What is the dog doing now?   _____
the ice cream

8   Listen and write the words.

| cow | mouse | ~~brown~~ | house | mouth | down | couch | town |

1 **2** **3** **4**

_____ brown _____ _____ _____ _____

5 **6** **7** **8**

sit _____ _____ _____ _____

9 Draw a town. Use these words.

| pet store | café | bookstore | hospital | apartment | park |

Me!

58

My picture dictionary

10   Complete the words. Stick.

① ap_a_rtment	② p__rk	③ st__re
④ h__sp__t__l	⑤ str____t	⑥ c__f__

My progress

Check (✔) or put an ✗.

I can talk about the town. ☐

I can write about the town. ☐

Marie's music   Animals in music

1   Listen and say the animal.

| a cat   a bird   a frog   an elephant   a sheep   a cow |

It's a bird.

They're cats.

Now you! **2**  Make a guitar.

 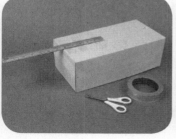 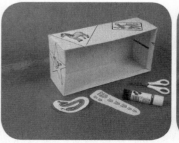 

3 Read and circle.

1. There's a **red** / **green** traffic light. You can cross the road.

2. Don't ride your skateboard **on the road** / **at the park**.

3. The sign says: **Don't walk** / **Walk** on the grass.

4. Put your **trash** / **books** in the trash can.

5. Don't cross the road. The traffic light is **green** / **red**.

4  Look and write "can" or "can't."

Do not walk on the grass.

1. I __can__ put my trash here.

2. I _____ walk here.

3. I _____ cross the road here.

4. I _____ play here.

Review

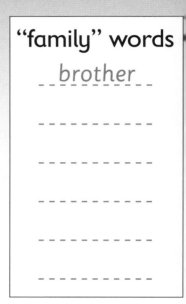

1 🔍 ✏️ Find and write the words.

"food" words
milk
_____
_____
_____
_____
_____

t g d r t y z x d j u
b r e a k f a s t u w
r a a m o m g y f i g
o n w n m c j x r c h
t d a d d t o s i e e
h m s l o i i i e k d
e o p a b h k s s s i
r t m m i l k t s m n
o h c k s o i e m g n
o e g g s j u r x k e
g r a n d f a t h e r

"family" words
brother
_____
_____
_____
_____
_____

2 ✏️ Listen and write the number.

 1

3 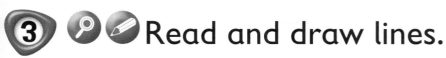 Read and draw lines.

The baby is behind the door.
The mother is between the bed and the desk.
The clock is on the bookcase, between the books.
The lamp is on the desk.
The polar bear is on the desk, in front of the lamp.
There's a spider under the bed.

4   Listen and complete. Chant.

Whose   Which   ~~Who~~   What   How many   Where   who   How old   What

① __Who__ is that?
That's my brother, Paul.

② _____'s he doing?
He's catching a ball.

③ _____ ball is it?
It's my cousin Nick's.

④ _____ is he?
He's very young.
He's only six.

⑤ _____ is he now?
He's in the hallway.

⑥ _____'s he doing?
He's throwing his ball.

⑦ _____ balls do you have?
I don't know!
We have a lot.

⑧ _____ one's your favorite – red or blue?
I don't know!

⑨ And _____ are you?

9 Our clothes

1  Listen and connect the dots.

2 Follow the "clothes" words.

watch	shoes	glasses	lizard	cake
thing	frog	socks	burger	sheep
hat	T-shirt	jeans	carrots	goat
pants	ice cream	cow	bread	spider
dress	skirt	jacket	shirt	purse

How many clothes are there? _____

Write the "animal" words. _____

Write the "food" words. _____

3 ✎ Write the words and color the picture.

a	b	c	d	e	f	g	h	i	j	k	l	m
☆	■	○	▭	◆	◧	●	★	◈	△	▼	◡	◑

n	o	p	q	r	s	t	u	v	w	x	y	z
◮	★	◤	◇	▲	◗	▽	□	▬	◡	▽	▭	◿

◈'◑ / ◡◆☆▲◈▲● / ■◡□◆ / △◆☆▲◗ , / ☆ /
I'm / _ _ _ _ _ _ _ / _ _ _ _ / _ _ _ _ _ , / _ /

▭◆◡◡☆◡ / ◡★◈▲▽ , / ●▲ ☆▭ /
_ _ _ _ _ _ / _ _ _ _ _ , / _ _ _ _ /

◡☆○▽◡ , / ■◡☆○▽ / ◡★☆◆◡ , /
_ _ _ _ _ , / _ _ _ _ _ / _ _ _ _ _ , /

☆▲▭ / ☆ / △◆◡ / ▲◆▭ / ★☆▽ .
_ _ _ / _ / _ _ _ / _ _ _ / _ _ _ .

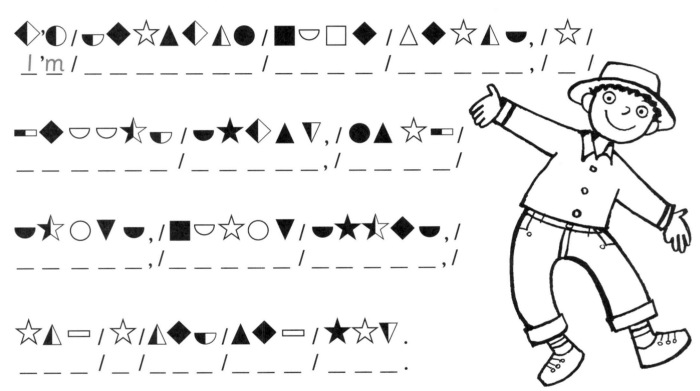

4 ✎ Describe your clothes.

Me!

I'm wearing _____

_____

_____

5 🔍✏️ Look and write.

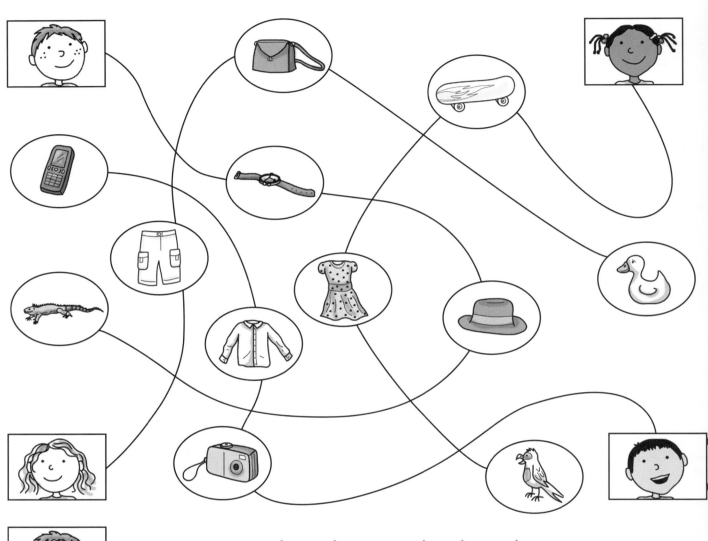

 I have *a watch, a hat, and a lizard.*

 I have _____

 I have _____

 I have _____

6 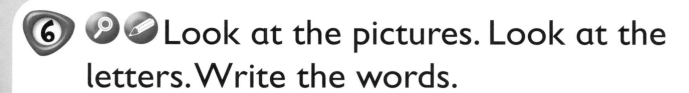 Look at the pictures. Look at the letters. Write the words.

Example

T-s h i r t

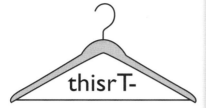
thisrT-

Questions

①

_ _ _ _ _

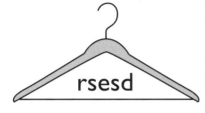
rsesd

②

_ _ _ _ _

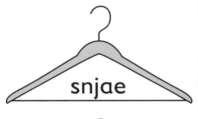
snjae

③

_ _ _ _ _ _

srtsho

④

_ _ _ _ _ _ _

ssslega

⑤

_ _ _ _ _

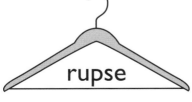
rupse

7 🔊 18 CD3 ✏️ **Listen and write *s* or *sh*.**

① _s h_eep

② ___oe

③ _even

④ sock_

⑤ __irt

⑥ de_k

⑦ fi___

⑧ dre___

⑨ _leep

⑩ _tore

8 🔍💬 **Cross out five objects.**
Ask your friend.

> Do you have a boot?

> Yes, I do.

hat	☐	lemon	☐
purse	☐	cow	☐
boot	✓	sheep	☐
glasses	☐	monster	☐
frog	☐	tomato	☐

My picture dictionary

  9 Listen and write. Stick.

1 _purse_	**2** ____	**3** ____
4 ____	**5** ____	**6** ____

My progress

Check (✓) or put an X.

I can talk about my clothes. ☐

I can talk about things I have. ☐

10 Our hobbies

1 ✏️ Write the words and the numbers.

① ② ③ ④ ⑤ ⑥

ptingain ___painting___ 4

btonadmin _____ ☐

ildef hokeyc _____ ☐

itagur _____ ☐

iPgn-ongP _____ ☐

ebbasall _____ ☐

2 🔵24 CD3 ✏️ Listen and color.

3 ✏️ Write the words.

Down ↓ Across →

3 **s w i m m i n g**

4 ✏️ Complete the sentences.

3 → They're _swimming._

4 ↓ She's _____

6 → She's _____

6 ↓ They're _____ _____

9 → He's _____

10 → They're _____ _____

5 🔊27 CD3 ✏️ Listen and check (✓) or put an **X**.

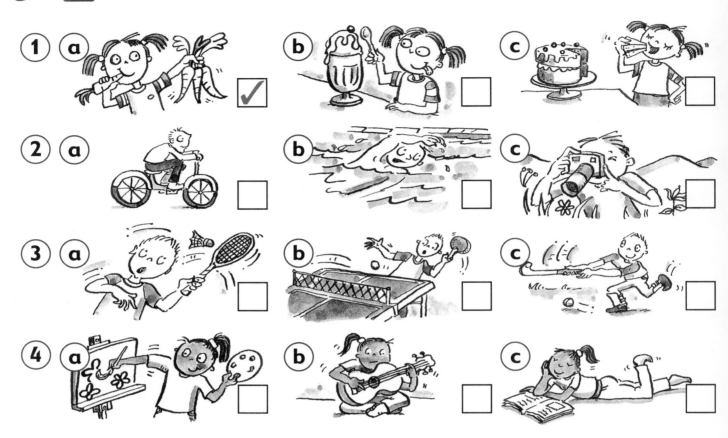

6 ✏️ Draw and write about you.

My name's _____ .

I'm _____ years old.

My hair is _____ .

My eyes are _____ .

My favorite toy is _____ .

I like _____ .

I don't like _____ .

I love _____ .

My favorite hobby is _____ .

Me!

7 🔍✏️ Look and read. Write "yes" or "no."

Example

Two boys are playing field hockey.   *yes*

A girl is playing tennis.   *no*

Questions

1. A boy is wearing a black T-shirt.   _____

2. Two boys are playing Ping-Pong.   _____

3. A tall girl is playing basketball.   _____

4. The boy under the tree is playing the guitar.   _____

5. A girl in a white skirt is playing badminton.   _____

8 🎧 31 CD3 ✏️ **Listen and match.**

1. A lo**ng** dog. _c_
2. The boy's eati**ng**. _____
3. She's si**ng**ing a so**ng**. _____
4. The ki**ng**'s readi**ng**. _____
5. She's painti**ng**. _____

a

b

c

d

e

9 🔍 ✏️ **Read. Write the words.**

Hi. I'm Tom. Now, I'm at
_____school_____ . I'm playing
_____ . I'm wearing
a red and white _____
and long blue _____ .
I like playing sports.
For lunch today, I have
some _____ and an
_____ . I like having
lunch at school.

74

10   Write the words. Stick.

bdanimtno	ginP-gonP	bsaeblal
badminton		
bakstebla	pniatngi	delfi oeyckh

 My progress

Check (✓) or put an X.

I can write "sport" and "hobby" words. ☐

I can talk about my likes. ☐

Marie's math · Venn diagrams

Now you! 1  Find, draw, and write.

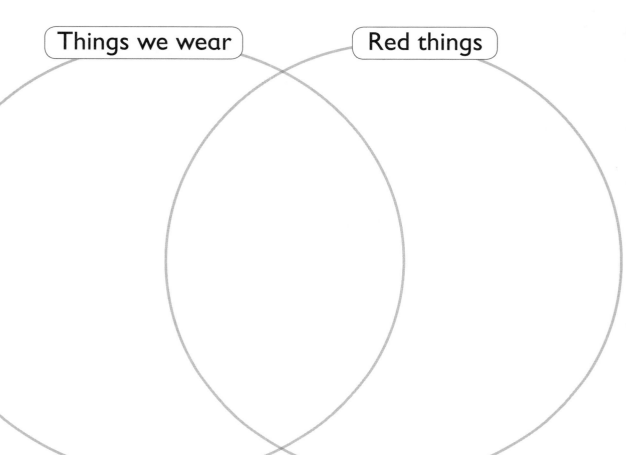

Things we wear

Red things

2 ✏ Write about your Venn diagram.

There are .... red things.

There are .... things we wear.

There are .... red things we wear.

3 Look and check (✓) or put an **✗**.

1

You can run with the ball.

Right rule? ☐

Wrong rule? ☐

2

You can throw the ball.

Right rule? ☐

Wrong rule? ☐

3

You can kick the ball.

Right rule? ☐

Wrong rule? ☐

4

You can hit the ball with a tennis racket.

Right rule? ☐

Wrong rule? ☐

4 Listen and say the sport.

It's basketball.

11 My birthday

1 ✏️ Write the letters and the words.

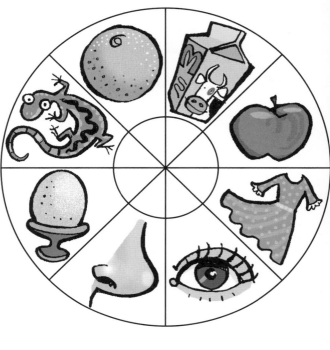

_ _ _ _ _ _ u _ _ _ _   _ _ _ _ _ _ _ _ _

2 🔍✏️ Circle the different words.

1 tree	yard	flower	(car)
2 shoe	camera	robot	kite
3 sausage	armchair	chicken	fries
4 lemonade	orange	milk	water
5 badminton	basketball	soccer	bus
6 café	desk	hospital	school
7 cupboard	bed	couch	kitchen
8 kitchen	hallway	bathroom	mirror

Listen and draw.

4   **Write the words.**

me	you	her	it	us	~~them~~

1

Look at ___them___ .

2

Can I play with _____ ?

3

Smile at _____ .

4

Take a picture of _____ .

5

Come and play with _____ .

6

Take a picture of _____ .

5 ✏️ Write the sentences.

① (fries?) (some) (Would) (like) (you)

Would you like some fries?
- -

② (some) (please.) (cake,) (like) (I'd)

- -

③ (Would) (like) (you) (to play) (us?) (with)

- -

④ (to play) (I'd) (Ping-Pong.) (like)

- -

6 🔍 ✏️ Read and write the information.

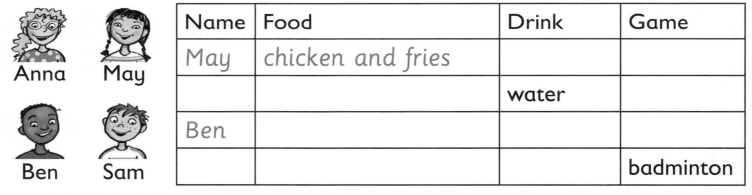

Name	Food	Drink	Game
May	chicken and fries		
		water	
Ben			
			badminton

Anna May Ben Sam

It's Anna's birthday, and she's having lunch with her three friends, May, Ben, and Sam.

① May would like some chicken and fries, and she'd like some orange juice.

② Ben would like some meatballs and potatoes.

③ One boy would like some sausages and tomatoes, and he'd like some water.

④ Two children would like some lemonade.

⑤ The two boys would like to play field hockey, and the two girls would like to play badminton.

⑥ One girl would like some carrots and rice. It's her birthday today.

7 Listen and draw lines. There is one example.

Tom   Jill   Dan   May

Mark   Hugo   Kim

Listen and write the words.

skirt	bird	~~purple~~	thirteen	burger	shirt	girl	birthday

①
_____purple_____

②
_____

③
_____

④
_____

⑤
_____

⑥
_____

⑦
_____

⑧
_____

⑨ **Look at the letters. Write words.**

Happy birthday, Scott.
It's your party today!

_____shirt_____   _____

_____   _____

_____   _____

_____   _____

_____   _____

_____   _____

My picture dictionary

10 CD3 49 ✏️ Listen and stick. Write the words.

① _cake_

② ____

③ ____

④ ____

⑤ ____

⑥ ____

My progress

Check (✓) or put an ✗.

I can ask for food and drink. ☐

I can talk about party food. ☐

12 On vacation!

1 🔺 🔍 Listen and check (✔). Find the words.

(1) ocean	✔	open	☐
(2) song	☐	sun	☐
(3) sand	☐	hand	☐
(4) shell	☐	she	☐
(5) mountain	☐	mouth	☐
(6) three	☐	tree	☐
(7) floors	☐	flowers	☐
(8) bird	☐	big	☐
(9) animals	☐	apples	☐
(10) phone	☐	fish	☐
(11) vacation	☐	train	☐

```
a  s  m  o  b  s  a  n  r
f  h  o  b  i  t  a  y  h
l  e  u  t  r  e  n  g  m
o  l  n  i  d  f  i  s  h
w  l  t  s  u  n  m  e  t
e  m  a  o  c  e  a  n  r
r  u  i  h  k  h  l  o  e
s  a  n  d  a  r  s  t  e
b  v  a  c  a  t  i  o  n
```

2 ✏ Match. Write the words.

o	ocean	old	cean	ld
b	_____	_____	eautiful	irt
m	_____	_____	ountain	un
s	_____	_____	and	each
sh	_____	_____	ell	ees
tr	_____	_____	ain	ouse

84

3 🔍✏️ Look at the picture and answer the questions.

1. How many people are there? _____*There are four people.*_____
2. What's the man drinking? _____
3. What's the woman doing? _____
4. Is the dog walking? _____
5. Where's the boy swimming? _____
6. What's the girl picking up? _____
7. How many birds are there? _____
8. Where's the jellyfish? _____

4 🔍✏️ Look at the letters and write the words.

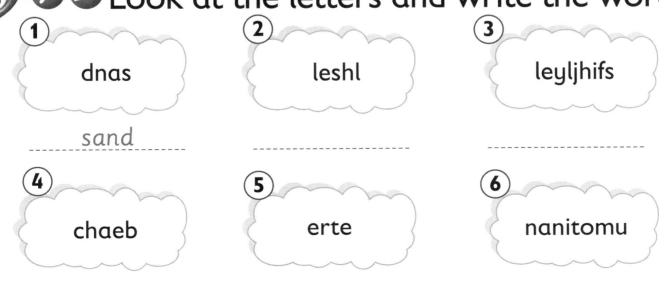

1. dnas

_____*sand*_____

2. leshl

_____

3. leyljhifs

_____

4. chaeb

_____

5. erte

_____

6. nanitomu

_____

5 🔊 CD4 ✏️ **Listen and check (✓) the box.**

1 What does Nick want to do?
  a ☐ b ✓ c ☐

2 What does Mary want to have for lunch?
  a ☐ b ☐ c ☐

3 What does Peter want for his birthday?
  a ☐ b ☐ c ☐

4 What does Susan want to drink?
  a ☐ b ☐ c ☐

5 What does Stacey want to play?
  a ☐ b ☐ c ☐

6 Where does John want to go?
  a ☐ b ☐ c ☐

6 🔍 ✏️ **Read. Write "Yes, he does" or "No, he doesn't."**

Daniel's birthday list
A cool skateboard   A new kite
A gray robot   A long ruler
A small camera   A chocolate cake

1 Does Daniel want a cool skateboard? _Yes, he does._

2 Does Daniel want a short ruler? _____

3 Does Daniel want a small kite? _____

4 Does Daniel want a gray robot? _____

5 Does Daniel want a small camera? _____

6 Does Daniel want some chocolate ice cream? _____

7 Listen and color. There is one example.

8 🔊 13 CD4 ✏️ Listen and match.

(1) Sam catches his ...   fish.
(2) Ben gets ...   stops
(3) Jill swims with the ...   hat.
(4) Tom ... the dog.   sun.
(5) Justine runs in the ...   shells.

(a) _2_   (b) ____   (c) ____   (d) ____   (e) ____

9 ✏️ Complete the questions. Then answer.

| ugly   new   short   ~~small~~   dirty |

(1) Is your kitchen big or _____small_____ ?

_____

(2) Is your city beautiful or _____ ?

_____

(3) Is your street long or _____ ?

_____

(4) Is your bedroom clean or _____ ?

_____

(5) Is your school old or _____ ?

_____

10   Complete the words. Stick.

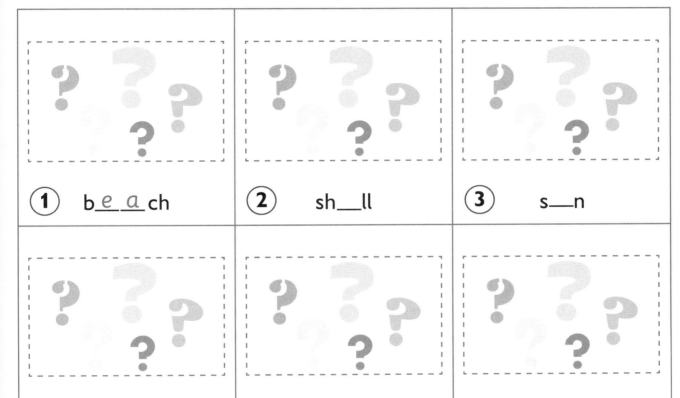

① b _e_ _a_ ch

② sh___ll

③ s___n

④ m_____nt_____n

⑤ s___nd

⑥ o_____

My progress

Check (✔) or put an ✗.

I can talk about my vacation. ☐

I can talk about what I want. ☐

Now you! **1** 🔍✏️ Read, draw, and color.

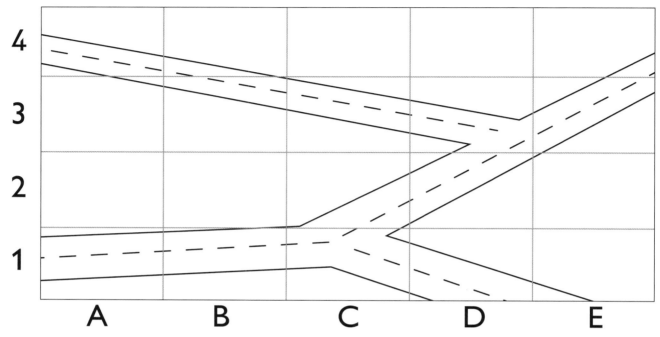

Draw a car in one square. Color it blue.
Draw a tree in one square. Color it brown and green.
Draw a flower in one square. Color it purple and green.
Draw a house in one square. Color it red.
Draw a mountain in one square. Color it gray.

2 💬✏️ Ask and answer. Draw.

Where is the car?

D4.

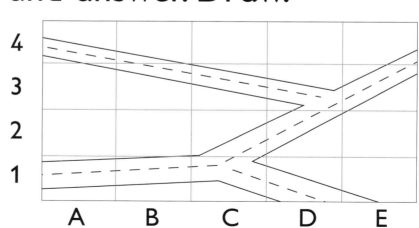

3  **Listen and write the number.**

4 **Write and draw.**

Me!

Review

1 🔊 20 CD4 ✏️ **Listen and connect the dots.**

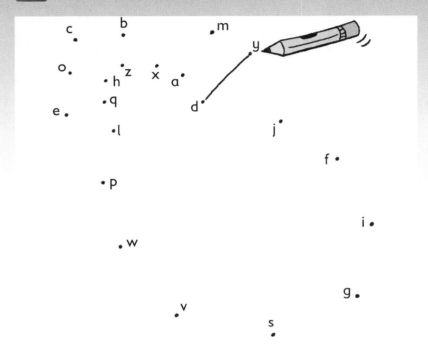

What's this? It's a _____ .

2 🔊 21 CD4 ✏️ **Listen and color. There is one example.**

3 🔍✏️ Match the questions and answers.

1. Whose shorts are they? **f**
2. Where are they playing badminton? ☐
3. Who's that? ☐
4. What color's your shirt? ☐
5. What's Mr. Star doing? ☐
6. Which dress is yours? ☐

a. He's cooking.
b. On the beach.
c. The long, red one.
d. It's green.
e. She's my cousin.
f. They're mine.

4 🔍✏️ Read and complete.

eat

→ 10

Grammar reference

1 Order the words.

① (Tom.) (What's) (his) (He's) (name?)

--------------------------- ? ---------------------------

② (Who's) (She's) (Mrs.) (Brown.) (my) (teacher,) (she?)

--------------------------- ? ---------------------------

2 Look and write.

Yes, there is.   Yes, there are.   No, there aren't.

① Is there a whiteboard on the wall? ✓ _____
② Are there three computers in the classroom? ✗ _____
③ Are there a lot of chairs in the classroom? ✓ _____

3 Circle the question and the answer.

Whoserobotisthis?It'sRobert's.

4 Match the questions and answers.

① Whose red dress is that?   Yes, they are.
② Whose blue pants are those?   It's mine.
③ Are those blue boots yours?   They're Dad's.

5 Look and complete.

'm not	'm	're	're not	's	's not

1. ✓ I _____ singing.
2. ✗ I _____ dancing.
3. ✓ You _____ reading.
4. ✗ He _____ running.
5. ✓ She _____ playing tennis.
6. ✗ We _____ painting.

6 Circle the question and the answer.

CanIhavesomefish,please?Hereyouare.

7 Look and write.

So do I.	I don't.	So do I.

1. I like rabbits.   ☺ _____
2. I like donkeys.   ☺ _____
3. I like spiders.   ☹ _____

8 Look and complete.

1. Where's the café?   It's **bhnide** _____ the school.
2. Where's the park?   It's **ni ofrnt fo** _____ the hospital.
3. Where's the store?   It's **teewenb** _____ the park and the apartments.

9 Write the answers.

| don't. does. doesn't. do. |

1. Do you have a skateboard?   ✓ Yes, I _____
2. Does he have red shorts?   ✗ No, he _____
3. Does she have a blue bag?   ✓ Yes, she _____
4. Do you have gray boots?   ✗ No, I _____

10 Look and complete.

| love   don't like   likes   doesn't like |

1. ❤ ❤   I _____ reading.
2. ❤   He _____ playing badminton.
3. ✗   She _____ singing.
4. ✗   I _____ cooking.

11 Look and complete.

| No, thank you.   Yes, please. |

1. Would you like some meatballs?   ✓ _____
2. Would you like some milk?   ✗ _____

12 Look and complete.

| I want to   I don't want to |

1. ☺ _____ go to the beach.
2. ☹ _____ go to a big city.

About me

School: --

Grade: --

Teacher: --

First language(s): ---

Other language(s): ---

Write your favorite words in different languages.

English

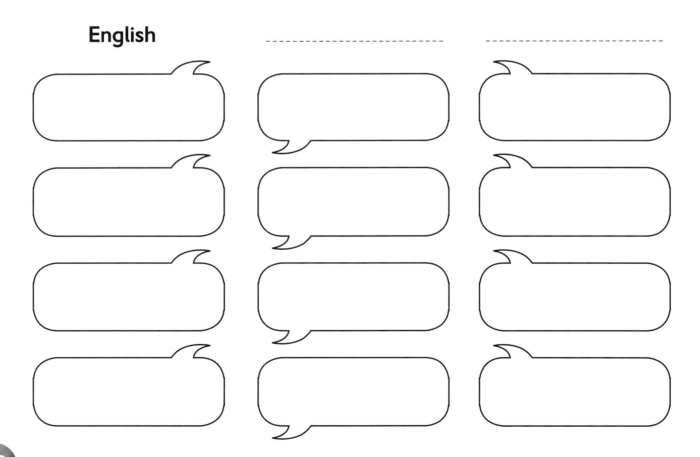

My language skills

1 Draw the pictures in the spaces below.

  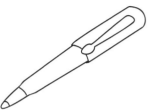 

Listening		☺
Reading		☺
Speaking	👄	☺
Writing		☺

2 Do you like doing these things in English?
  Color the faces. Blue = It's good. Green = It's OK.

I can ... # Units 1-3

1 Listen and color.

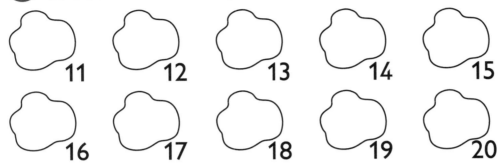

11   12   13   14   15

16   17   18   19   20

2 How do you spell ...?

3 Read and match.

camera   bike   truck   robot   computer game   kite

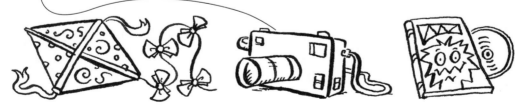

4 Write.

My favorite toys are _____

_____ .

1

2

3

4

I can ...   Units 4-6

1 Listen and point.

1 ☺

2 💬 Tell your partner about your family.

My family is small. I have ...

2 ☺

3 🔍 Read and match.

bread   water   juice   fries   chicken   rice   egg   milk

   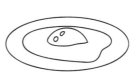

3 ☺

4 ✏️ Write about your favorite lunch.

----

4 ☺

I can ... Units 7–9

1 🎧 **Listen and point.**

2 💬 **Point and say.**
Use "in," "on," "next to," "under," and "between."

3 🔍 **Look at the picture. Check (✓) or cross (✗) the boxes.**

1 The park is between the toy store and the café. ✗
2 There's a doll and a car in the toy store. ☐
3 There's a street and there's a park. ☐
4 The monkey is under the tree. ☐
5 There's a hospital next to the café. ☐
6 The ball is on the table. ☐

4 ✏️ **Write about your favorite clothes.**

102

Color the face: I can do it!
1
2 😊
3 😊
4

I can... Units 10-12

Color the face: I can do it!

1 Listen. Say "yes" or "no."

1
☺

2 Point and say.

2
☺

3 Read and circle the pictures above.

What would Ben like?

I'd like some lemonade and a sausage. Oh, and I'd like some watermelon, please!

3
☺

4 Write.

I can see _____

and _____ in the mountains.

I can see _____

and _____ at the beach.

4
☺

English and me

I learn English …

… in school ☑

… at home (private classes) ☐

… at an academy ☐

… in the summer ☐

My favorite English activities are:

listening ☐ reading ☐ speaking ☐ writing ☐
games ☐ songs ☐ using the book ☐

I speak English to my _____ .

An English song I like: _____

An English book I like: _____

An English movie I like: _____

People speak English in _____ .
I want to go there on vacation!

My school bag

Draw your school bag. What's inside it?
Color your picture.

My school bag

Now write about your school bag.

My bedroom

Draw or stick a picture of your bedroom.

My bedroom

Do you have these things in your bedroom?
Write "yes" or "no."

phone _____ mirror _____ armchair _____ guitar _____

bookcase _____ computer _____ cupboard _____ toys _____

lamp _____ rug _____ clock _____ window _____

What do you have in your bedroom?

My family

Draw or stick a picture of you and your family.

My family

The people in my picture are:

How old are they?

My _____ is _____ years old.

My _____ is _____ years old.

Things I love

Draw or stick pictures of things you love.

I love ...

My favorite food is _____ .

My favorite sport is _____ .

My favorite animal is _____ .

My favorite _____ is _____ .

I love _____ !

My favorite clothes

Draw or stick pictures of your favourite clothes.

My favorite T-shirt.   My favorite shoes.

My favorite _____ • _____ •

A vacation

Draw or stick a picture from your vacation.

My vacation

What people, things, and places are in your picture?

Write about your vacation.

Thanks and Acknowledgments

Authors' thanks

Many thanks to everyone at Cambridge University Press and in particular to:

Rosemary Bradley for supervising the whole project and for her keen editorial eye;
Emily Hird for her energy, enthusiasm, and enormous organisational capacity;
Colin Sage for his good ideas and helpful suggestions;
Claire Appleyard for her editorial contribution.

Many thanks to Karen Elliot for her expertise and enthusiasm in the writing of the Phonics sections.

We would also like to thank all our pupils and colleagues at Star English, El Palmar, Murcia, and especially Jim Kelly and Julie Woodman for their help and suggestions at various stages of the project.

Dedications

I would like to dedicate this book to the women who have been my pillars of strength: Milagros Marín, Sara de Alba, Elia Navarro, and Maricarmen Balsalobre - CN

To Paloma, for her love, encouragement, and unwavering support. Thanks. - MT

The Authors and Publishers would like to thank the following teachers for their help in reviewing the material and for the invaluable feedback they provided:

Alice Matovich, Cecilia Sanchez, Florencia Durante, Maria Loe Antigona, Argentina; Erica Santos, Brazil; Ma Xin, Ren Xiaochi, China; Albeiro Monsalve Marin, Colombia; Agata Jankiewicz, Poland; Maria Antonia Castro, Spain; Catherine Taylor, Turkey.

The authors and publishers would like to thank the following consultants for their invaluable feedback:

Coralyn Bradshaw, Pippa Mayfield, Hilary Ratcliff, Melanie Williams.

We would also like to thank all the teachers who allowed us to observe their classes and who gave up their invaluable time for interviews and focus groups.

The authors and publishers are grateful to the following illustrators:

Adrian Barclay c/o Beehive; Andrew Hennessey; Beatrice Costamagna, c/o Pickled ink; Chris Garbutt, c/o Arena; Emily Skinner, c/o Graham-Cameron Illustration; Gary Swift; James Elston, c/o Syvlie Poggio; Kelly Kennedy, c/o Syvlie Poggio; Lisa Smith; Lisa Williams, c/o Syvlie Poggio; Marie Simpson, c/o Pickled ink; Matt Ward, c/o Beehive; Melanie Sharp, c/o Syvlie Poggio.

The authors and publishers acknowledge the following sources of copyright material and are grateful for the permissions granted. While every effort has been made, it has not always been possible to identify the sources of all the material used or to trace all copyright holders. If any omissions are brought to our notice, we will be happy to include the appropriate acknowledgments on reprinting.

p.17 (background): Thinkstock; p.31 (background): Thinkstock; p.45 (background): Thinkstock; p.60 (sheep): Shutterstock/chaoss; p.60 (bird): Shutterstock/Kutlayev Dmitry; p.60 (frog): Shutterstock/Alfredo Maiquez; p.60 (elephant): Shutterstock/Johan Swanepoel; p.60 (cow): Shutterstock/Martin Nemec; p.60 (cat): Shutterstock/elwynn; p.61(background): Thinkstock; p.77 (background): Thinkstock; p.91 (background): Thinkstock.

Commissioned photography on page 60 by Trevor Clifford Photography.

The publishers are grateful to the following contributors:

Louise Edgeworth: picture research and art direction
Wild Apple Design Ltd: page design
Blooberry: additional design
Lon Chan: cover design
John Green and Tim Woolf, TEFL Audio: audio recordings
John Marshall Media, Inc. and Lisa Hutchins: audio recordings for the American English edition
Robert Lee: song writing
hyphen S.A.: publishing management, American English edition